It Seemed Innocent Enough

WalkerDoodle Press

Also by Art Elser

We Leave the Safety of the Sea

A Death at Tollgate Creek

As The Crow Flies

To See a World in a Grain of Sand

Memoir

What's It All About, Alfie?

It Seemed Innocent Enough

Poems

Art Elser

WalkerDoodle Press

Copyright © 2019 Art Elser
All rights reserved.

No part of this book may be reproduced or transmitted in any form or by any means, electronic or mechanical, including photocopying, recording, or by any information storage and retrieval system without the expressed written permission of the author, except in the case of brief quotations in critical articles and reviews.

ISBN-978-0-9984554-6-4

Cover Photo by Bruno Cervera on Unsplash.

WalkerDoodle Press
Denver, CO 80220

As always for Kate

I wake in love
on our anniversary
thirty-seven years

Acknowledgements

These journals and anthologies have previously published the poems listed, some in slightly different versions:

300 Days of Sun: In the Silence of the Canyon.

Celestial Musings: Poems Inspired by the Night Sky: In a Minnesota Summer Night, 1974; To See a World in a Grain of Sand; Night Sky, Sand Dunes, July 1987.

Emerging Voices: Even in Death You Would Not Share, Religion of Fear.

High Plains Register: Warm Morning on a City Sidewalk, We Called It Crossing the Fence.

NFSPS Encore: My Father Died While Shoveling Snow.

Open Window Review: Elegy for the Dinosaurs.

Poems from the Back Forty: At the Corner of Colfax and Krameria.

Quill & Parchment: At a Once Abandoned Cattle Ranch.

Red Coyote: A Brief Scent of Rain, Four Massive Horses Stand Quietly.

Sequestrum: Meditation on the Death of a Spider, Only the Bones Are the Same.

Serendipity Poets Journal: Aerial Perspective, You Have to Know It's There.

The Avocet: Brown Spider in a Leaf, Rain After Years of Drought, Peaceful Morning's Walk, You Ask Where I Come From.

The Human Touch: Narcotic Shape Shifters.

The Weekly Avocet: An Old Enemy Invades the Mob's Neighborhood; Asheville Days: A Haiku Series; Oh Dear, What Shall I Wear?

Contents

Acknowledgements iv
It Seemed Innocent Enough 1
As I Wait for My Non-fat Latte 2
Thursday Morning at the Coffee Shop 3
Choosing from the Sunday Lunch Menu 4
Warm Morning on a City Sidewalk 5
At the Corner of Colfax and Krameria 6
Meditation on the Death of a Spider 7
Letter to a Friend Dying from Brain Cancer 8
Notes from a Very Strange Summer 9
Religion of Fear 10
Eurydice Waits 11
Aerial Perspective 12
Thoughts On the Change of Seasons 13
You Ask Where I Come From 14
Scenes from a Recurring Dream 15
Narcotic Shape Shifters 16
Make Hay While the Sun Shines 17
The Ballad of Malcolm P. Dragon 18
Oh Dear, What Shall I Wear? 19
The Decal in the Rear Window 20
My Father Died While Shoveling Snow 22
His Reflection in a Darkened Window 23
White Sheets on a Clothesline 24
Even in Death You Would Not Share 25

When Friends Have Asked Me	26
Your Tree Is Almost Dead, And Yet,	27
A Poet's Deep Purple Funk	28
Wildflowers	30
On Seeing A Girl I Once Dated in a Painting	31
Four Massive Horses Stand Quietly	32
Questions from a Painter's Studio	33
What Does He Read There?	34
Saturday Morning Run	35
If You Sit Still Long Enough in Nature	36
As I Put Some Books Back on the Shelf	38
The World Is Charged with the Grandeur of God	40
Autumn Rains Come Early	41
Rain After Years Of Drought	42
October 5th, 2017, 8:30 PM	43
Elegy For The Dinosaurs	44
Brown Spider in a Leaf	45
How Meadowlark Got Its Song	46
The Deep End of the Sky	48
Coyote's Prayer to the Great Spirit	50
The Homestead	51
Last of the Homesteaders	52
At a Once-Abandoned Cattle Ranch	53
Only the Bones Are the Same	54
You have to know it's there	55
Epiphany on a Blue School Bus	56
Seriously, What Are the Chances?	57

We Called It Crossing the Fence	58
Asheville Days: A haiku series	60
A Prairie Sunrise	61
In a Minnesota Summer Night 1974	62
A Brief Scent of Rain	63
Afternoon at an Old Farm Pond	64
An Old Enemy Invades the Mob's Neighborhood	65
In Search of Solitude for Inspiration	66
In the Silence of the Canyon	67
The Last Dragonfly of Summer	68
Beauty Found on Our Morning Walk	69
Peaceful Morning's Walk	70
Night Sky, Sand Dunes, July 1987	71
The Light on the First Day of September	72
About the Author	73

*Tell me, what is it you plan to do
with your one wild and precious life?*

        Mary Oliver "The Summer Day"

It Seemed Innocent Enough

A man and woman in their 70s sit in the dark,
sipping coffee. Lightning flashes from a line
of thunderstorms to the west of Bahía Banderas,
where the bay meets the ocean. Lightning splashes
off the black waters of the bay, but the thunder
barely growls in the pre-dawn quiet.

He remarks that the lightning makes him think
of the first morning that life was created. How the
lightning sparked life in volcanic primordial stew.
She nods but doesn't reply.
                        After a bit she says
the lightning reminds her of sparks at a party
they attended forty years before.

      She sat alone—her husband playing water polo.
      He also alone—his wife had begged off the party.
      At first he wasn't sure who she was, sitting there,
      alone. She didn't remember him.
                            Both had changed
      since they last met. And when he asked to join her,
      she nodded yes. They struck sparks that night
      as they chatted by themselves for a few hours.

As dawn comes to the bay, steam rises from
jungled slopes where rain had fallen earlier.
Small fishing vessels inch their way out
to the mouth of the bay. Pelicans skim
the waves. Frigate birds grace the blue
above the bay. Couples stroll the beach.

They laugh as they sip their coffee, talk
about the sparks struck that night. How old lives
ended as they created this love-filled new one.

As I Wait for My Non-fat Latte

He sits, back to me, leaning slightly toward her.
He talks softly. She does not speak. Her sad
gray eyes look near him, but not at him.
Her posture, her sagging body leaning away,
her stricken look, say that his words are painful,
words she did not think she would ever hear.

Does he explain why he has been unfaithful,
why he wants to move out for now, forever,
why he sees no future to their relationship?

He looks away from her, down at his phone.
She leans forward, takes a napkin from the table,
dabs her wounded eyes, leans back, broken.

My drink order is called and I look away.
As I walk to my car I cannot help but wonder
how his feelings for her have somehow gone,
how he has caused the terrible pain in her eyes,
how I'm to deal with this sadness in my heart.

Thursday Morning at the Coffee Shop

Two women sit at the table in front of me,
their service dog curled up next to them.
As women normally do, they face each other
directly as they speak, but with a difference.
Their hands speak to their eyes.

The waitress brings menus. The older woman
asks for coffee and signs to the other, relaying
the waitress's questions. They read the menu,
point to choices, exchange suggestions, and chat,
hands flitting like chickadees carrying messages.

When the waitress comes back, the older woman
again speaks as the younger watches intently.
The waitress leaves and their hands ramble on
about what the rest of us can only wonder at.

The dog watches with loving eyes, follows
the back and forth of their conversation.
I wonder if he knows what they say?

Choosing from the Sunday Lunch Menu

A man in his sixties in bib overalls holds open the door
as an older white-haired woman strides in and points
to a booth with her dark cane. His large calloused hands
gently place the large menu into her small arthritic ones.
She reads intently, eyes searching, mouth working, as if
she tastes each dish, then announces she'll have the spaghetti.
He feigns surprise—it's what she's had for Sunday lunches
the past dozen years. When her plate comes, she whispers,
"I'll eat half and take the rest home for supper." The waitress
winks at him and sets down a take-home box before he asks,
as she has for Sunday lunches for more than a dozen years.

Warm Morning on a City Sidewalk

An old, homeless woman stands rooted,
huddled in a worn red parka, oblivious
of the morning heat. She studies something
in her right hand.

As I get nearer, I look to see what coin,
small note, or snapshot holds her rapt attention.
I see only the ragged, too-large work glove
she wears, its fingers splayed at broken,
arthritic angles.

I don't realize I'm staring until she lifts her head,
and gray, vacant eyes peer into mine.
Embarrassed, I hurry across the street,
glance back to see if she watches me.

My rudeness, though, is no match
for the mystery of that glove.

At the Corner of Colfax and Krameria

An old man, fringe of curly gray hair peeking out
from his blue baseball cap, waits for the walk light
before starting across six lanes of traffic at rush hour.

When the signal changes, he starts, first lowering
the wheels of his walker by feel the six inches down
to the road, then lowering his own fragile weight.

All eyes follow his slow lurching progress as he moves
across first one lane then two then three. He doesn't
stop at the safety of the median but continues on.

Cars turning left, wait for him to reach the center strip
before slowly going. The light changes. Nothing moves,
no one honks, drivers watch his slow, painful journey.

He reaches the curb, climbs onto it, first the walker,
then his weight, painfully, one foot then the other.
Cars slowly drive on. We begin again to breathe.

Meditation on the Death of a Spider

As I shave, I reflexively swat at a tickle on my hip
and crush a tiny spider crawling there. Was he there
because I walked through his web and caught him up
or was he blown there by the breeze of my passing?
His death means little to me, but I do offer an apology,
saying his death was accidental, without my intent.

As I think on that spider's death it seems little different
from the drunk driver who doesn't see the stop sign,
hits a car killing a mother, her three-year-old daughter,
sparing her son who will grow up without his mother,
leaving her partner who will grieve for their deaths.

What kind of God allows this senseless mayhem
to destroy lives? Does this God cause or allow
the earthquake that devastates a poor island,
killing hundreds of thousands of sleeping people,
or a tsunami that kills tens of thousands more?
And the wars. Oh God! The never ending wars.

How can I square these events with the all-loving,
all-knowing, all-powerful God of my catechism?
The God who knows when a single sparrow falls,
dresses the lilies of the fields in their spring finery.

Why does this God allow gratuitous violence to take
the lives of so many of his children, dooming those
who love them to lives of grief? Does he not care?
Is he not there? Have we had it wrong all this time?

Did the Greeks, thousands of years ago, get it right,
the three Fates determine our destiny, one spinning
life's thread, one measuring it, and one shearing it,
as I sheared the thread of that tiny spider's life?

Letter to a Friend Dying from Brain Cancer

You've had this inoperable brain cancer now
for some time but have stayed mostly ahead
of its debilitating effects until these past weeks.

That marvelous brain that allowed your body
to guide jet airliners across the world's oceans,
while carrying people's hopes, dreams, lives.

And now your sense of balance goes off kilter,
the strength in your legs goes, so you can no
longer safely climb stairs or pedal your bike.

The bike you rode each year a hundred miles
across Death Valley to raise money for research
to find a cure for your son's juvenile diabetes.

The bike whose wheel you dipped in the Pacific,
climbed the high Sierras and Rockies, pedaled
the continent east to dip a wheel in the Atlantic.

Your past feats of will, endurance, and courage
have been fine exemplars to us who know you,
encouraging us to make the most of our lives.

And now in the face of an uncertain future, we
who watch and follow the steps of your decline,
find it difficult to accept that you'll soon be gone.

So as you continue your battle, despite knowing
that death must come finally to us all, I wish you
Godspeed, *Vaya con Dios* on your final flight west.

Notes from a Very Strange Summer

Today low thunder and short showers as we lurch
through a summer full of drought-fueled wildfires
that have destroyed homes, lives, national forests.
Great floods as Noah-like rains keep falling, falling,

drowning streets, homes, neighborhoods, villages,
all brought on by global warming that disrupts
our normal weather patterns. The smoke from fires
in the drought-stricken west makes breathing hard.

Meanwhile the cancer growing in your brain disrupts
your normal summer, tipping your balance, making
your muscles weak, forcing you to take long sleeps.
I suspect cancer soon will make your breathing hard.

Almost half this year to go. but your year hurries by,
seasons racing at you too quickly. Will your year come
to its end early, while ours continues on without you
into seasons that seem hell bent on destroying all?

Religion of Fear

When I was nine, one summer afternoon
each week, I was sent to catechism class
where humorless nuns marched us
to a beautiful grotto set in a hillside,
framed by maples, oaks, and flowers.
The grotto had a small statue of Mary
in a blue robe, holding the baby Jesus.

The nuns lectured us about God's love.
But, if I whispered or squirmed, one
of the nuns would come up silently,
grab an ear and twist or yank a handful
of hair and warn that I'd burn in hell.
Those nuns, Darth Vader prototypes,
in their black habits and starched wimples,
stormed imperially across my childhood.

Why didn't they show us the beauty
of the flowers by that peaceful grotto?
Why didn't they point to the trees
and tell us how they nurtured birds?
What if they had sat quietly with us to listen
to chickadees, orioles, cicadas, crickets?
What if they had showed us God's creation?

Would that have changed my childhood faith?
My spiritual life? How would I believe today?

Eurydice Waits

Affrighted by the wails of barely seen
shades, raging and howling in a darkness
that is visible, tangible, I wait on the shore
of this black river for the ferryman to come.

I had, as Persephone commanded, followed
Orpheus up that path, out of the underworld.
I saw him emerge into starlight, saw his joy,
for that instant, as he turned his face to me.

In that instant, the starlight blinked out,
the pathway ended, and a voice in me
raged in terrible pain, pain worse even
than the viper's bite on my wedding day.

So I wait, assailed by the dreadful shrieks
from innumerable writhing, faceless dead,
stare into the lapping blackness of the river,
hear the slow rhythmic oar of the ferryman.

And in this sulfurous dark I hear, far off,
Orpheus's lyre, playing a sorrowful dirge,
knowing his backward glance doomed me
to this eternal, howling, raging underworld.

Aerial Perspective

He watches the sun slide down
toward the Laramie mountains
twenty miles to the west. The valleys,
ridges, and peaks are softened
by a haze that gives form
and distance and grace to them.
The prairie is lush from a wet
spring and summer and the low
sun paints seed stalks gold,
and deepens the green of the grass.

The sunset reminds him that his life's journey
too is nearing its end--he has already used more
than his allotted three score and ten. And his life
has been graced by a light that gives form
and definition to its valleys, ridges, and peaks,
a light that glows golden on the fruitfulness
of his days.

The sunset dims to alpenglow.
The beauty and grace of that moment
assures him that *his* light
has been well spent.

Thoughts on the Change of Seasons

I stop, look around as my pup painstakingly sniffs
a bush, and notice the neighbor's crocus are up but
not yet unfurled. I listen to a choir of finches sing
from nearby elms whose buds have begun to swell.

The approach of spring brings, of course, an end
to winter. I've seen more than 82 winters now and
wonder if my life's own winter will also soon pass,
wonder what the coming *terra incognita* will be like.

Will it be a Christian looked-for-end to a vale of tears,
an elevation to a heaven of angels and golden streets,
or an intermediate stop where my soul will wait until
I've been pardoned for a life's plethora of petty sins?

Will it be a Hindu reincarnation, in a different form,
one determined by how enlightened I was in this life;
will it be in human form again or perhaps as an insect—
one that flies I hope—if that's a choice that I'm allowed.

Will I walk the Cheyenne long fork of the Milky Way
to join my friends in the camp of the dead, or will I ride,
like the Navajo, a spirit horse into their land of the dead,
a world they believe very similar to the one we're in now.

I'm not much for formal religion or rituals, I think perhaps
this world with its purple crocus blooms; its finchy choirs;
the immensity of its starry sky; its wonder, beauty, and joy;
is enough for me. The pup tugs the leash and we move on.

You Ask Where I Come From

> *a mote of dust suspended in a sunbeam*
> Carl Sagan, from *Pale Blue Dot*

Billions of years ago in a place far, far away
a creative genius took a small, dense black ball
and flung it against a brick wall in his back yard.

The ball exploded with a big bang, and clouds
of fiery dust scattered in all directions, lighting
the sky as they raced into the emptiness of space.

Some of the dust clung to other pieces of dust and
as each piece gathered more burning dust to itself
it formed stars, then galaxies with billions of stars.

Much later, some of those stars became too dense
and hot and exploded just as the original dark ball
had exploded, creating more huge clouds of dust.

That dust traveled through the space the creator
and his neighbors now call the Universe because
it has gotten so large. And star filled. And beautiful.

The dust from those exploding stars from all over
the Universe, traveled past other stars that had spun
off small planets and moons that were not burning.

As the dust fell on those new planets and moons,
some fell on a planet called Earth and magically
gathered into combinations now called life forms.

One of those life forms on the planet Earth is called
human, and since I am human, where I come from
is easy to answer. I come from stardust.

Scenes from a Recurring Dream

I wonder if this is what it feels like, the loss
of orientation as one grows older. It happens
to me in dreams. I'm flying over hostile terrain
familiar to me in my dream, not when awake.

Then slowly, the scene morphs until I don't
recognize it any more. Suddenly shot at.
I don't know how to get from this place
that I don't know to a place that I do, to safety.

Over the years the dream itself has morphed
to one less dangerous, but no less frightening.
I'm in an alien land with people I do not know.
I try to go home. I'm lost. I'm in *terra incognita*.

I wonder if this is what Alzheimer's feels like?

Narcotic Shape Shifters

I sit in my hospital bed and watch a squadron
of silver shape shifters fly out of the room
and stop behind the nurses station. There
they form precise ranks as they pass in review
and then hover in flights ready for a mission.
I send my wife and kids out to look at them,
but they are unable to see them. They shake
their heads and look at me as if I'm crazy.
Another line of larger shapes drifts
into my room and lands on the ceiling
to form baroque patterns that look
like streets in some futuristic city.

Later that evening, the night nurse
comes into the room, and I show her
the detailed patterns on the ceiling
and the flight of large metallic shapes
flying in to create intricate patterns.
She does not see them either, so I have her
come close to the bed where I can point
to the patterns. Again, she doesn't see them.
But unlike my family, she looks at me
with knowing concern and tells me that I
am hallucinating from the anesthesia and drugs
the doctors have given me over the past week.

I'm dismayed that the shapes are phantoms
of my drugged mind. But I sit back, smile,
and enjoy the magic air show.

Make Hay While the Sun Shines

I worked on a farm that summer as a young man.
One day we got the hay into the barn by the skin
of our teeth. Rain came down like cats and dogs.

The boss's daughter gave me that come hither look
and climbed the ladder to the hay loft. Never slow
on the uptake, I climbed too. There we made hay.

Several months later, her call scared me to death.
Said she was in the family way, said her daddy
was fit to be tied, mad as a hornet, a raging bull.

Not one for shotgun weddings, I pulled up stakes
and got out of Dodge. Headed west young man
where buffalo roam, deer and the antelope play.

I put all my eggs in one basket and flew the coop.
A long story short, I disappeared into thin air,
figuring there's more than one way to skin a cat.

As luck would have it, I got the short end of the stick.
Her dad caught up with me and dragged me back
kicking and screaming. We lived happily ever after.

Some advice: don't make hay while the sun shines.
Save up for a rainy day, and vanish without a trace.
But above all, avoid using clichés like the plague.

The Ballad of Malcolm P. Dragon

Each morn near nine, my Lady Bright Eyes,
I call her that, but she's really Lady Eileen,
rides up on her roan mare and calls sweetly
at the mouth of my cave, "Malcolm, I'm here."

I wait inside not wanting to seem too eager.
So I come out slowly and kneel at her feet.
She pets my head and asks if I will heat
the water for her tea, an herbal tea, I think.

She sets the kettle on an iron stand and I
breathe gently on it for some little time.
And as we wait for it to boil My Lady sings
songs of love and scratches behind my ears.

Today some bloody fool in a shiny tin suit
galloped in on a huge black horse and yelled,
"I'll save you My Lady!" and ran his lance
through my neck, pinning me to the ground.

He got off his horse, drew his sharp sword,
and threatened to lop off my head. My Lady
Bright Eyes, yelled "Stop! Stop! Desist fool!"
then gently knelt beside my head and cried.

Her tears fall into the gathering pool of my
chocolate brown life. And as my flames cool
and sight begins to dim, I hear My Lady cry
and sing a sweet sad song of a dragon's love.

Oh Dear, What Shall I Wear?

Mother Nature walks to and fro, eyeing clothes in her closet.
She no longer wants to wear the reds, burnt oranges, golds,
tawny, umber tones of fall. She loved their muted colors

after the deep greens and all of summer's bright colors. But
she also loved the lime green of spring's new leaves, lilacs,
crocuses, the bright red and gold tulips, the yellow ranks

of daffodils. She's tired of them all and wants a change.
She slides to her right, hesitates, looks for something new,
walks to the far end of the closet, pulls out a black dress,

black as deep space, spangled with stars, narrow black straps.
Imagines herself dancing away winter's blahs on cold nights,
their crisp air, star-bright snowfields, in this little black dress.

The Decal in the Rear Window

My father was yanked from high school
in September of '24, as he turned fourteen,
two weeks after starting his freshman year.

His father, a master bricklayer, arranged
for another master to take him on as his
new apprentice for the next three years.

The WPA started after Dad was certified,
so he laid many perfect rows of bricks
for city buildings during the depression.

His career blown up by Japanese bombs
in December of '41, he apprenticed again,
this time to make airplanes for the Navy.

He became proficient in this trade quickly,
and soon rubbed shoulders with engineers
who designed the airplanes that he built.

At dinner he would regale us with how he
had told an engineer that day a new design
would not work and tests proved him right.

When I went to college at MIT, with plans
to be an engineer, he got a decal from there
and put it in the rear window of his car.

Even after I flunked out and went elsewhere
to get a degree in English, that decal stayed,
through changes of cars every three years.

For many years I was sure that the decal
was his angry jab at me for not becoming
the engineer that he was never able to be.

When he retired and got another new car,
he didn't put the decal in the rear window.
Looking back, these three decades now,

I think perhaps the decal was to avoid
the question, *Where did you go to school?*

My Father Died While Shoveling Snow

It's odd that I thought of him dying that way
at eighty-three, as I shoveled snow this morning.
I almost never think of him. I can't remember
shoveling snow with my father.

I do remember snowy days, riding my sled
in front of the house, after cars had packed
the road hard and icy and fast.
I'd run, boots sliding, and belly flop
on the sled to enjoy the long glide.
And pulling the sled to Pond Path to ride
down that long hill. Look up and down
for cars before I'd run and flop
to a fast slide. Fun! Even the long,
sweaty trudge back up to do it again.

I remember afternoons with my sister
when we were teens, walking to a pond,
miles from home. We'd scrape the snow
from the ice and skate for hours. Then the tired,
laughing walks home in the gathering dark.
And knee-deep, snowy walks to school,
the ice on the ditch at Kennedy's hill;
I thought it would hold me, but it never did.
So I'd squish to school wahooing, sliding,
galoshes filled with ice-cold slush.

But for the life of me, I can't remember
shoveling snow with my father.

His Reflection in a Darkened Window

He looks into the dark December night,
at scattered ranch and farm lights, thinks
about the lives of people living there. Then
his own reflection startles him, makes him
ask how he feels about his father's death.

Never close, his father showed little interest
in his son's life, his successes, his failures.
He was not mean, not outwardly, but was
in his aloofness to family, daughter-in-law,
grandchildren, their lives, their loves.

He reflects on the grief friends have shared
on the loss of parents, in never talking with
or seeing them again, wonders what's wrong
that he doesn't feel. Has his father's aloofness
somehow rubbed off on him?

He is sad, not that he will never see him again,
not that he will never hear him laugh again.
His sadness comes from realizing that he feels
no grief for the man, who, with his mother,
gave him life, nor guilt for not feeling grief.

When he's home he tries to comfort his mother.
She says curtly, "Your father is in a better place."
He is confused at what this says about her grief.
Were they, in sixty years of marriage, also aloof?
Or is her calmness a mask, her grief yet to come?

White Sheets on a Clothesline

The sheets fluttered there mid-morning,
white flags signaling Mom's surrender
to the custom of washing on Monday.
She would first add wood to the black
iron stove and then walk next door
to pump buckets of water. She would
heat it and pour it into the galvanized tub
(the one we bathed in on Saturday night).
In the kitchen, a glass washboard, a bar
of Ivory soap on its wooden divider,
waited for her.

She scrubbed until she was convinced
a piece was clean enough for neighbors
to see, then twist it with bright red hands,
wringing out soapy water as if she were
wringing a chicken's neck. Then, heating
more water, she rinsed clothes and sheets,
put them in a wicker basket, carried them
to the clothesline behind our house.
In winter, clothes froze as she hung them
on the line. So did her hands.

I was a child and most of the clothes hung
well above my head, where I couldn't
reach them. But the clean, white sheets
hung low, and I could bury my face in them
and inhale their fresh, country-air smell.
That is the scent of my childhood.

Even in Death You Would Not Share

I sat all morning at your bed,
held your hand, told you it was alright
for you to go, reminded you that you
had often said you wanted to be with Dad,
even when you could not remember
that he had died a dozen years before.

I'd been home half an hour
when the phone rang.
I knew that you had died.
I knew, from seventy years
of being your child,
that you would not share
your death with me.
I knew you would have said
you did not want to put me
through those emotions.

When I entered your room, I saw
that the aide had brushed your hair,
changed your gown to a flowered one,
folded your arms upon your breast.
The pain lines on your face were gone.
You looked peaceful and content.
Content that you had succeeded
in keeping me from sharing that final
and sacred moment of your life.

When Friends Have Asked Me

After Lisel Mueller

When friends have asked me how I came
to poetry, I've usually lied to them. I've told
I wrote to free myself of pain and guilt
from time at war, flashbacks that I had.

But I came to writing poetry more quietly,
from my grief the night that Nanny died.

I sat in a chair in the next room as she slept,
keeping watch, attending to her needs.
I dozed, then woke, startled by a harsh rattle,
and knew that now her death was near.

I nodded off and woke hours later to silence,
broken only by a lonesome cricket's chant.
The cricket stilled. I listened for her breath.

Then the wind chime above the barely
open window softly, very softly, tolled
the passing of her soul. Then silence.

I allayed my grief with paper and pen,
setting it to that night's soft, soft music
of a wind chime that tolled grief's start.

Your Tree Is Almost Dead, And Yet,

this morning sunlight dances on a patch
of bright leaves surrounded by gnarled
spare webs of branches that are dead.

Three years it has borne no fruit, and yet,
each spring its arms are filled with blooms
that get nipped by mid-spring arctic gusts.

For many years your tree bore too much fruit.
We had to cull the many peaches growing there
so heavy freighted branches wouldn't break.

And now your tree is almost dead, and yet,
it makes us smile. Its hold on life reminds
us of your peace and joy and love.

A Poet's Deep Purple Funk

The plan was to use *color* as the prompt
to trigger the inspiration to write a poem.
So I start to think on some colors I know.

I first seize on the brownness of the prairie,
its pronghorns, prairie dogs, coyotes, grass,
and then the spring-gold swaths of wallflower,
patches of lavender penstemon, thistles, white
glow of sand lilies, daisies, dusty green sage
but nothing comes, nothing pops, I am stuck.

Then I think of the deep gray, almost black
shadows of Bach's *Toccata and Fugue*, thundered
from a huge church organ, or its silver to copper
notes, breathed from a flute in a simple church.
But again nothing, I remain stuck.

Maybe Beethoven's *Sixth Symphony* with its bright
red tulips, yellow fields of Wordsworth's daffodils,
lime green cottonwoods along a creek in spring,
pale blue columbine in a sunny mountain meadow,
the delicate pink of the tiny, secretive fairy slipper.
And yet the same nothingness and still stuck.

Perhaps Samuel Barber's quiet *Adagio for Strings*
with its deep blues and violets from that far end
of the rainbow's spectrum, its black-red terrors
of the Vietnam War for Charlie Sheen in *Platoon*.
Or the sunset's magenta silences in the adagio
of Mozart's *Clarinet Concerto in A* as Redford
and Streep dance the night away in *Out of Africa*.
Again, no inspiration. Dead in brackish water.

So I'm a frustrated poet in a deep purple funk,
pen poised over white paper, black ink waiting,
and no colorful poem to show for all my trying.

Wildflowers

after Connie Wanek's "Blackbirds at Dusk"

We fell in love in wildflowers, a field of them
ablaze with penstemon, lupine, copper mallow,
that waved so gently in the sun-kissed breeze.

Though penstemon and purple lupine
look to have mouths and tongues
and nodded silently as we kissed,

we knew that they would never tell.
Since that sweet kiss, the world has turned
from love to rage and fear and hate.

But still each spring the wildflowers bloom
and wave to us as we pass by.

On Seeing A Girl I Once Dated in a Painting

When I first see the Cassatt painting of a woman
with a pearl necklace at the Paris Opera, I'm stunned
to remember your red hair, the freckles on your Irish
white skin, that look of love's promise on your face.

We were just kids, you 17 and me 19, but we knew
we were in love. I flew off to college, you met Charlie,
fell in love again, married the boy from the junkyard.
I wonder where you are, what your life has been like.

Are you still there in that little village, a grandmother,
with children of your own? Is Charlie still working
with junked cars? Or did he strike it big, with smart
moves using the wrecks in his yard to make a fortune?

Has life transported you from the wrath of your mother,
the fears that you would never escape into a normal life?
Could you be that woman in the loge of the Paris Opera
with that string of pearls, smiling with self-contentment?

Do you ever think of the boy who wanted to fly, to see
the world from above? If so, do you ever wonder, what
became of him, as I wonder now and then about you?
I hope that you now wear a beautiful pearl necklace.

Four Massive Horses Stand Quietly

The Tower of Blue Horses—Franz Marc

Four massive horses stand quietly
in the blue shadows of a summer sunrise.
Gold light filters through cottonwoods
and dapples their searching faces.

They wait for the young girl who comes
to them each morning in this meadow
with apples, carrots, and happy smiles.
Her voice sings with the meadowlark's.

The horses might have stepped this day
from a cave at Lascaux, painted there
twelve thousand years ago by the hand
of this girl in the softness of her dreams.

Questions from a Painter's Studio

on The Girl with the Pearl Earring

The natural light in the painter's studio,
shines softly on the young girl's face,
setting it off from the dark background,

framing it in the blue of her turban and
muted gold of her robe and white collar.
It shines bright only in her eyes and pearl.

Did Vermeer fall in love with the girl
as he watched her dress, while posing her,
or was he already smitten with her charm,

so he chose her to sit for him that day?
Do her eyes show wonder at his fame, or
smugness knowing she's captured his heart?

Do her eyes mirror a love in Vermeer's eyes,
his heart astonished by her beauty, or do we
see that beauty only by his skill as a painter?

Mona Lisa enigma. Do we see her as she was,
as the painter saw her, or as he wanted us
to see her so we'd be captivated too?

What Does He Read There?

My dog loves history and studies it
every day as we walk the avenue.
He scans many books, new and old,

with his acutely tuned senses and then
stops to read a long passage in a book
he finds of interest. When he's satisfied

he's gotten the sense of the story straight,
he blesses it with his special holy water
and quickly moves on to the next book.

As we walk I often wonder out loud
when he's spending a long time reading
a patch of a neighbor's lawn or tree trunk,

if he reads about a dog living nearby
or a tale of some prehistoric dire wolf
who roamed here during the last ice age.

Saturday Morning Run

I whistle for Tara, our husky, who comes running,
clip on her leash, struggle against her eager pull.
Across the lawn, down the street, right turn
on the boulevard, run along cement sidewalks.

After a mile and a half, all up hill, we come
to where the pavement ends. I slip her leash.
More uphill through those sweet scented fields
of waving prairie grass, dotted with grazing cows.

Where the road levels a bit, at the cut in the ridge,
I see green meadows where prairie blends with hills.
Tara sometimes sees and plays there with coyotes.
She seems half wild, seems almost to be one of them.

A short level stretch of Wilson Road, hard packed dirt,
and then up the twisting curves of that long steep hill.
Around a curve one morning a startled red angus bull
threatens until Tara nips him and barks him off the road.

Then straining to the top of that long pull, legs aching,
we turn at the pavement, head back down to home.
We lope easily, again through the cut in the ridge.
I put the leash back on, and soon Beethoven begins.

In my head, an orchestra plays, a loud German chorus
sings *Ode to Joy* matching my pace. And joy fills my day.

If You Sit Still Long Enough in Nature

the gods may smile on you, but you must
be quiet, make all your movements slow
and next to your body, so you become
a large rock or a mound of earth.

Once, on a quiet, sunny, September morning
the gods conjured Coyote out of wheatgrass,
down the slope from where I was sitting quietly,
absorbing the nature around me. Coyote appeared
suddenly, cutting across the faint trail I had used
to get to the depression that once had been the well
for a homestead where I sat, feet dangling.

Coyote stopped, froze, looked at me with frightened
eyes. I spoke softly to her, told her I meant no harm,
that she was beautiful, thanked her for visiting me.
She relaxed and trotted off rather than bolting,
running, fleeing. I think the gods were pleased
and smiled on me again some weeks later.

I walked the prairie to a low spot that blocked view
of most signs of man's hand and sounds of his activity.
I sat on a cut bank by a dirt road, became a mound
of grass, leaned against a rock, closed my eyes, took in
the peace of the morning, smell of grass, scent of sage
I had walked through, the sun's warmth on my face,
the tingle of soft wind on my arms.

My body slowed its rhythms, breathing, beating
of my heart, and I opened my eyes. I turned
ever so slowly to see what the prairie might offer.
A movement at the top of a low ridge north of me
caught my eye. A pronghorn buck grazed at the top
of the ridge. I watch as he became six, nine, twenty,
thirty-six pronghorns moving slowly toward me.

Ahead of the main herd was a doe and two fawns, fawns born but four months before, just half the size of their mother. They still wore the spots of youth. Like children in a toy aisle, the fawns moved faster than the herd, their mother keeping up to make sure they were safe. They came within thirty yards of me.

I dared not speak for fear of spooking the entire herd, and worried that they would walk right into me. The buck leading the herd, or the gods, turned the herd and they ambled their way back up and over the ridge. Once again the gods had smiled on me.

As I Put Some Books Back on the Shelf

books I'd pulled off the bookshelf months before
to reread, I come across Mary Oliver's *House of Light*,
a book that 25 years ago shaped my life as a poet.

I had just started writing poetry, and when I first read
Oliver's poems in *House of Light*, they captured my heart
with their images like those in "Some Herons":

> *A blue preacher / flew toward the swamp / in slow motion.*
>
> *On the leafy banks, / an old Chinese poet /*
> *hunched in the white gown of his wings.*
>
> *The water was the kind of dark silk / that had silver lines /*
> *shot through it / when it is touched by the wind /*

I marveled at how at the end of this poem she merged all
the images of the swamp as blue preacher, Chinese poet,
and dark water come together.

> *They entered the water / and instantly two more herons —/*
> *equally as beautiful / joined them and stood just beneath them.*

And in another poem Oliver describes two does she sees
in the woods, walking like two mute / and beautiful women.
The does walk toward the poet, one almost touching her
as she waits quietly. Her response:

> *I was thinking: / so this is how you swim inward, /*
> *so this is how you flow outward, / so this is how you pray.*

I was moved by her deep reverence for nature,
and she helped me discover my own reverence.

Back then I was at a point in my poetic life in which "two roads diverged in a yellow wood," so I felt that I must answer her question in "The Summer Day."

> *Tell me, what is it you plan to do*
> *with your one wild and precious life?*

I want to try to write poetry as beautiful as yours about my love for life and our wonderful world.

The World Is Charged with the Grandeur of God

after Gerard Manley Hopkins

September's green turns ochre, red, and gold,
as southbound geese fly past in noisy Vees.
The days get short as nights grow long and cold.

Red combines harvest swaths of golden wheat
and apple tree limbs droop with ripened fruit
as summer's green turns ochre, red, and gold.

High meadows fill with sounds of bugling elk
and children search throughout the pumpkin patch
for one to carve as nights grow long and cold.

Neat gardens prized for multicolored blooms
are now but withered stalks and shriveled vines.
They fill with leaves of ochre, red, and gold.

The feeders hum with finch and chickadees.
And bears spend weeks binge eating to get set
to hibernate as nights grow long and cold.

Autumn days fill with the grandeur of God
as we await the star-bright winter skies.
The trees burn bright with ochre, red, and gold
but soon the wintry nights grow long and cold.

Autumn Rains Come Early

> *There will come soft rains*
> *and the smell of the ground*

Dawn splays a high deck
of cirrocumulus clouds
across the droughty sky,
sheep on distant blue hills.

Later the clouds curdle
to buttermilk, cradle a pale
quarter moon, then hide it
in a wallow of low clouds.

Finches and chickadees
at the feeder all morning,
grab their fill. Then wind
picks up, sends them off.

Rain starts slowly, evenly,
falling all day, never hard.
Petunias in the side yard,
dance all day in their joy.

Rain After Years Of Drought

A soft change to the silence of the night
awakens me. Rain against the window.
The luscious smell of falling rain in the air.
It's the first rain we've had in two years.

Sudden memories of listening to rain
in my bedroom as a child. Summer nights
watching lightning and counting seconds
until the thunder rolls in. I snuggle down

into the covers and listen for a long while,
then drift into sleep. I awaken hours later
to the same delicious sound and smell,
the answer to prayers of farmers, ranchers.

Now we pray that this rain will be the first
of many and break this long drought.

October 5th, 2017, 8:30 PM

High thin clouds fade from light pink to gray,
and cumulus on the etched black mountains
burn a fiery red, as the sun slides down.

In the east the night spreads its dark wings
and a hawk glides to his roost on a cottonwood.
A pair of nighthawks starts their dusk patrol.

A nearby meadowlark finishes his evensong,
and all but a solitary cricket joins the hush.
As dark creeps farther west, a soft light stirs

in the east and the gold harvest moon eases
over the horizon, lighting the silent scene.
In the cottonwoods by the creek, an owl hoots.

Its mate hoots back softly. A lone coyote from
a den beyond the creek, yips twice and throws
a long, quavering howl into the prairie night.

Elegy For The Dinosaurs

A flaming asteroid from darkest space
crashes into the sea near Yucatan.
It hits at fifty thousand miles an hour.

It causes earthquakes, huge tsunami waves,
a supersonic blast of burning gas
that flies across the surface of the earth

so ancient forests and savannahs burn.
A giant cloud of shattered rock and dirt
is thrown into the sky and blocks the sun.

The rage of fire and chill of prolonged cold
kills off the mighty dinosaurs and leaves
the Earth to try mammalian life this time.

Don't grieve though. Dinosaurs exist today
in dreams of boys and girls with whom they play.

Brown Spider in a Leaf

Diamonds of morning rain glisten
on a spider's web spun across coils
of a garden hose next to the house.
The raindrops highlight the random
structure of the web, their weight
dragging down the threads
so carefully set.

In a leaf from a nearby ash, dry, curled
and wedged between the wall and hose,
hides a brown spider who sits, head-down
in the leaf, resting because its web
is too visible and not likely to snare
anything. The spider stretches his legs,
lifting his body, ready to run from me.
Today has not begun as a good one for him.

How Meadowlark Got Its Song

One day as Raven flew over the village,
he saw a Navajo maiden fetching water.
He landed on a tree close to her and saw
that she was as beautiful as the dawn sky,
as lithe as the willows in the creek, eyes
bright as a harvest moon, black as onyx.

Raven, the creator and trickster, fell in love
with the beautiful maiden, changed himself
into a tall, dark-eyed, young Navajo man.
He met the young maiden and tricked her
into falling in love with him. Then he saw
Coyote eating a rabbit and grew hungry.
He changed back into Raven, flew away,
stole the rabbit, and forgot the maiden.

The maiden grew sad as she could not find
the young man she had fallen in love with.
Each morning as she walked from the village
to the creek, she sang a song so sad that others
became sad. Soon the whole village grew sad.
Nothing the maiden's mother or father did
made her happy so they asked the shaman
to take away the maiden's great sadness,
make her onyx eyes smile brightly again.

The shaman talked to the maiden, suspected
Raven had tricked her, so he summoned Raven
to the village. When Raven saw her sadness
and heard her mournful song, he too grew sad.
So he changed her into Meadowlark, gave her
a beautiful song to sing each morning. Her song
cheered her mother and father and the village.

He gave her a gold breast and black necklace
so everyone would always find her beautiful.

If you listen carefully to Meadowlark's song,
you will hear a slight note of sadness in it.

The Deep End of the Sky

The warbling calls of a flock of cranes
reaches down to the woman and her son
as she fills buffalo bladders in the creek.

> *Mother, what are those cries like those*
> *of rabbits when father's arrows hit them*
> *and they cry out in fear until they die?*
>
> *My son, those are the crane spirit voices*
> *calling to the buffalo spirits to let them know*
> *that the prairie is green and the creek runs.*

She bids her son to follow as she hefts
the bladders to her shoulders and starts
toward the tipis on the spring-green hill.

That afternoon the boy runs to his mother
when he hears thunder in the prairie sky
as storms roll off the far-away mountains.

> *Mother, what is that loud booming sound*
> *that causes me to fear? A frightful sound*
> *as if many horses stampede around us.*
>
> *Those are the sounds, my son, of storm gods*
> *calling to the buffalo spirits, inviting them*
> *to come to this green hillside and this creek.*
>
> *Mother, will I be afraid when the buffalo come?*
> *You may be afraid, my son, because the ground*
> *will shake under your feet and rumble in your ears.*
>
> *And will you and father also be afraid, Mother?*
> *Your father is brave and will not fear, but I will*
> *fear as he races his pony alongside the buffalo.*

That night the men build a fire. They dance and pray to the buffalo spirits. Then they paint their faces and ponies for the hunt.

In the morning the thunder rolls, the ground shakes. That night the Cheyenne eat meat of buffalo that the hunters have killed.

Coyote's Prayer to the Great Spirit

Oh Great Spirit, thank you for giving me
these four fine pups, a mate who hunts well
and daily keeps us in food. And thank you
for keeping the pups safe from hunting eagles.

Please grant me the wisdom to raise the pups
so as they learn to hunt on their own, they never
forget to thank the prairie dogs, rabbits, voles,
and mice for giving their bodies to us as food.

Please grant me the wisdom to teach them how
to hunt well, find good mates, select den sites
that are safe from dangers like the two-legged
animal and his dogs, and to raise good pups.

Please also let them hear me thanking you
for the many blessings you have bestowed
on us, so they learn that they should also
thank you for blessings on their families.

Please help my mate find food enough today
so that the pups grow big and help us stay
healthy and strong. Great Spirit, thank you
once more for all your blessings in our lives.

The Homestead

A faint trail leads up from
the shadowed dry creek
to sunlight on a grassy ridge.
Three faint small depressions

in the grass mark what once
was a homestead house.
I pick up a chipped rusty
kettle and pour sand from it.

A snarl of rusted barbed wire
is the only other evidence
that someone once lived
on the land. Old timers say

that a widow and three sons
lived here. They raised cattle
and tilled a vegetable garden.
Nothing tells what happened

to them. I gently set the kettle
in the grass and follow the trail
back to the creek in fading light.

Last of the Homesteaders

A large old cottonwood stands alone
in the corner of a small grassy field.
Oddly it's here in the middle of the city,
surrounded by people, blacktop, buildings.
It is massive, more than a century old.

Why is it here, far from creek or pond?
Was there once a homestead here, the tree
part of a wind break planted by a family
trying to scratch out a living in soil too weak,
weather too dry for their crops, their hopes?

Did they give up, move away, leaving only
this tree to mark their failed sojourn here?

At a Once-Abandoned Cattle Ranch

I sit among blanched bones of an old ranch
and hear the absence of cows bawling,
horses neighing, the slam of pickup doors,
the grind of a tractor haying in the meadow.
There seems only silence until I listen.

                          Then I hear
the final notes of a distant meadowlark's song,
rattle of a kingfisher, hovering over the North Fork,
chitter of cliff swallows scooping bugs from the air,
whine of mosquitos in my ear. The wind so soft
it makes no sound and barely cools my arm
where the sun warms it.

                    Thump of thunder
from a storm whose virga skirts almost reach
the ridge a few miles west, the whistle of a woman
calling her dog, and between these few sounds,
the bright silence of the mountain-high prairie.

Only the Bones Are the Same

with a nod to Wislawa Szymborska

Suppose I met that young man whose picture hangs
in the back hall. In it he stands tall, cocky, jauntily
leaning against his airplane, small though it is,
his hand resting easily on the pistol at his side.
He's clear eyed and smiling.

Suppose he asked me to sit with him in a coffee shop.
How would I feel this half century later about him
and the things that he did?

Would I be awed by the fearlessness of his days,
or would I be angry that he didn't give a damn
about saving time for me so I could live a full life?

Would I shake my head at his naiveté, believing
the lies his president told? Or would I be proud
of his conviction in doing what his country asked
of him? Proud of his willingness to die for the men
he supported on the ground?

Would I be appalled at his quick elation in killing,
not thinking about the mothers, wives, children,
families who would never see those men again?
Or would his saving the lives of his countrymen
balance his lack of grief over the lives he took?

I'm sure he was unaware then of the pain and grief
and guilt I later would feel for the things he had done.
But I am glad that he has passed on to me his sense
of honor and integrity wedded to these same bones.

You have to know it's there

to find the rock, hidden as it is, in the woods
where a twelve-year-old boy and his grandma
sit on it in the sun, laughing and playing —
the boy scampering up and down its sides.

This truck-sized piece of granite has rested here
for many years as shown by the dense forest
of large trees surrounding it and the patches
of green and yellow lichen that grow on it.

Twenty thousand years ago a quarter-mile-thick,
slowly moving glacier wrenched this boulder
from continental bedrock twenty miles north,
grinding and rolling it to the top of this hill.

But to the boy and his grandma, these facts
are not important. They climb the gray rock,
scaling its scarred and pitted sides, to rest
and eat jelly sandwiches in the warm sun.

This is not their first adventure here together.
His grandma brings him here every summer,
leading them on the long – long for a child –
trek through the blueberry-filled woods.

They cannot know now that twenty years later
the boy will return from war in pain, haunted
by nightmares filled with terror, chaos, guilt,
and screams of agony from dying comrades.

Memories, however, of his grandma's laugh,
the sun's warmth as they sat on that boulder
will have the power one day, like the glacier's,
to roll away his pain, the darkness and despair.

Epiphany on a Blue School Bus

I'm tired. The air is putrid, hot, an assault of foreign smells.
My B-4 bag feels heavier than yesterday when I packed it.
I wrestle it up the steps onto the bus, stagger five rows back,
drop the bag, and plunk down next to an open window.

A rusting, heavy steel mesh on the window doesn't block
my view as we edge onto Saigon's noisy, crowded streets.
The breeze through the mesh, although it's hot and tastes
of oily diesel and moped fumes, cools my face and arms.

We unhurriedly make our way toward Bien Hoa Air Base,
my unit headquarters, where they'll assign me up north.
I'm excited, have romantic daydreams of battles, my bravery,
showing my naivete and ignorance. I'm finally going to war.

We slow to a crawl, stopping frequently, inching through
a teeming open-air market with its stink of human filth,
rotting meat, fish, vegetables, shouts of vendors bartering
with women who buy weekly groceries for their families.

Suddenly, I'm aware that many of the people in the market
wear black pajamas and conical straw hats, that ubiquitous
uniform we've learned that the Viet Cong wear into battle.
I grasp now why the open windows are protected by mesh.

Taller, fairer than the locals, I'll stand out, unable to hide.
My daydreams vanish, replaced by a feeling of vulnerability.
Fear settles into my bones, will live there for the next year,
flood, crescendo at times, then ebb, but never, ever to leave.

Seriously, What Are the Chances?

It's to be a normal reconnaissance mission,
Dick to check me out on a new area in Laos.
So, the flight starts with a simple question:
"Which seat do you want?" He answers "Left."

Rescue helicopters and fighters circle ahead
over a valley, and then the second question:
"Can we help?" Answer "Yes, can you check
the weather in the valley before we go down?"

So we sneak down through a small hole
in monsoon clouds to check the weather
to help them save two fliers shot down
the day before by enemy guns in the area.

We fly through the valley twice, looking
for the downed pilots. Just as we see them,
we're hit by gunfire. A loud noise, violence,
sudden shock, blood, horror, confusion.

A bullet hits Dick in the head, but he wears
a ceramic helmet given him by an Army pilot.
The helmet deflects the bullet, saves his life.
His is the only ceramic one in our squadron.

If his answer had been "Right," I would have
been sitting in the left. That bullet would have
gone through my head. Christmas Day, 1967.
Is this God's gift, my luck, fate, or just chance?

We Called It Crossing the Fence

that squiggly line on the map showing where
the French had divided Vietnam from Laos
many years before. It runs the crest of a ridge
under triple-canopy jungle. From the air it was
impossible to see because there's nothing there.

It was a strange war. The US said we weren't
in Laos at all. North Vietnam also said they
weren't there. So I was not really there, and
that was good because the NVA guns
that weren't there couldn't hit my plane
that also wasn't there.

At night we'd cross the fence to find trucks
not driving along the Ho Chi Minh Trail,
which also wasn't there. We had fighters
drop bombs on trucks, but the drivers
were spared death because they also
weren't there.

There was another fence, one dividing Laos,
Vietnam, and Cambodia from each other, more
imaginary lines on the map drawn by the French.
Guns that weren't in Cambodia shot at me, who
wasn't in Laos, scaring me as if I were there.

And US Army guns at Dak To—they were there
because on the east side of the fence—fired at night
on the NVA who weren't there on one side of the fence
but who were suddenly there on the other. Once I
was back over the fence, I was there again,
so the Army guns came close to shooting me down.

A strange war. Did I lose anyone along the way?
On which side of the fence did I lose you?
Are you sure you're there?

Asheville Days: A haiku series

clouds catch fire
over ancient mountain ridge
Asheville sunrise

light climbs ridge
fog slips into valley
stretches . . . sleeps

yesterday's ridge
wandered off in the night
foggy morning

blue ridge parkway
winds through hardwood forests
imagine autumn

one sits . . . calm
one calls . . . with whole body
two crows

shadow flits
across my journal page
hides in tree

black with flashing blue
winging the mountain meadow
spicebush swallowtail

two bumble bees
fondle dandelions
mountain meadow

far blue ridges
softened by the soft blush
of sunset

A Prairie Sunrise

I stand in the dark, coffee mug warm in my hands,
easing the winter numbness from my fingers.
I'm comfy in my parka as I watch the thin light,
first barely visible, edge onto the eastern horizon.
Then it torches the edges of a band of gray clouds
into flame. The clouds turn a deep blood red,
as if the whole prairie were alight with wildfire.

Mind drifts back 57 years to the 3 AM darkness
of a cold November night. I watch blood red flames
reflect off smoke from the burning airplane hulk
I've just crawled out of. Another, not so lucky, dead.
Medics check my lungs for smoke damage, my body
for burns, bruises, turn me loose to go home to rest.

Thoughts of my mortality wander through sunrise
as the blood red pales to cerise, like the red fingers
of tracer bullets, 50 years ago, that reach out for me,
for my little plane. They are so close I can hear
them pass, snapping wildly by the open window.
I am certain I will die on this pale Vietnamese day.

As the sun clears the horizon and the cloud bands
fade to pale gray, the sky sparkles to a lupine blue
as it was 6 years ago when my heart decided to quit.
An ambulance ride, heart jump-started by EMTs
and doctors in the ER, a triple bypass, three weeks
in the hospital. But today my heart lub-dubs along.

My meditation's broken by chick a dee dee dees
from the peach tree as three tiny black and white
birds flit from bare branch to feeder and back.
I give thanks for this cold winter morning, its gifts:
a prairie sunrise, some cheery birdsong, my life.

In a Minnesota Summer Night 1974

I lie on my back facing north in my sleeping bag
and watch a star-brilliant night sky, the Milky Way,
wandering off to the southwest with its millions of stars.

I can not find the big bear, lost in millions of galaxies.
I fall asleep, awaken hours later, the sky finely laced
with gauzy dancing clouds. Puzzled until I realize

that I watch the *aurora borealis*, sheer, graceful, green
curtains, blowing in the cold Minnesota sky, solar wind
made visible. The silent dance continues, shimmering,

expanding, contracting in the star-filled universe.
I feel dizzy, off balance in an out-of-kilter world.
I press my arms to the earth to keep from tumbling.

A Brief Scent of Rain

The sky closed down, dark and thick.
Wind hissed in the trees and they danced.
The finches at the feeders flew to a nearby
ash, except for one who perched briefly
on a wire and sang. A squirrel on the wall
ducked out of sight.

The day cooled and filled with the scent
of rain. The hiss of the wind in the trees
became the hiss of a hard rain on leaves
and grass. A faint mist tickled my arms.

The afternoon seemed somehow to change,
trees moved closer, backyard grew smaller.
The sound of the rain drowned the racket
of traffic and the city. Twenty minutes later
the rain slacked, city noises intruded again,
and the finches returned to the feeders.

But that brief scent of rain took me to a small
meadow thirty years ago, a hastily set up tent
that my son and I crawled into as a hard rain
started pelting it as thunder had been pelting
our ears for an hour. We lay on sleeping bags,
and fell asleep to that sound on the tent fly
and the hiss of rain on mountain ponderosa.

Afternoon at an Old Farm Pond

The blue heron stands at attention,
immobile, at the edge of the pond.
The heron's yellow legs blend with
the pale reeds. A cruising sunfish,

looking for a meal, sees a fat worm
wriggle in the mud of the shallows.
The fish swims cautiously closer,
knowing that danger often lurks

near the pond's edge. It slowly fins
into the shallows. It stops and looks.
The heron continues wriggling its toe
to bring the fish closer, and slowly,

almost imperceptibly, slides its head,
curves its neck into position to strike,
to spear the wary fish. The slow dance
continues. The fish, peril not perceived,

draws closer, the heron stops, steadies,
a bow drawn taut to release an arrow.
The lightning-quick thrust cleanly spears
the unsuspecting, now thrashing sunfish.

The heron tosses the fish, catches it
head first, swallows, and walks away,
its tautness released, its hunger sated.
The old farm pond, once again, calm.

An Old Enemy Invades the Mob's Neighborhood

The owl sits on a branch near the top of a spruce
where needles and gloom are thick. It is hidden,
invisible to the crows who fly in bright sunshine.

But the crows have discovered the owl is in there.
A brave crow lands on a branch near the owl, peers
into the gloom. Sees nothing, but hears it hiss.

The leader of the mob yells and curses as crows
quiet, land in nearby trees, tire of the long chase.
Exhorted to action, the crows again fly, scream.

The older crows tire, knowing the owl is not going
to come out and fight. They will not enter the gloom
so fly to their roosts, leaving the mob to continue.

The late fall afternoon fades quickly and the gloom
spreads from the trunk to the tips of the branches.
Soon more crows fly off leaving only youngsters.

Then they instinctively realize the owl is dangerous.
They have seen the river of black feathers in the wind
flowing from the gloom of a tall spruce. They leave.

Finally in the quiet of the evening gloom, the owl
closes its eyes, sleeps, dreams of catching a crow,
tearing flesh, creating a river of black feathers.

In Search of Solitude for Inspiration

Out on the prairie, I stop at a trail I use
but find it is closed, so I drive on, park,
and wander a seldom-used trail loop.

I'm immediately distracted by a butterfly,
a Juvenal's duskywing, fondling a thistle,
then many of them, and a single monarch

who sips nectar from a prairie sunflower.
Not to be distracted by more butterflies,
I walk away, find a bench to sit on, rest,

find solitude. I let the constant drone
of cicadas from a stand of scrub oak
become white noise, close my eyes,

slow my breathing, clear my mind.
I open my eyes and see a doe and fawn
who have stepped from the scrub oak.

My heart races as I watch them amble
along in the prairie grasses. When I
stand to watch them, they run away.

Realizing that inspiration from solitude,
isn't in the cards for me today, I leave,
happy with the beauty that I've found.

In the Silence of the Canyon

The tall, sun-parched prairie grass
no longer swishes on my pant legs,
now the crunch of boots on scree
muted on the hard-packed canyon trail.

Hot and sweaty from the long trek,
I joy in the canyon's quiet shade,
find a large rock to sit on, and take
a long drink of my lukewarm water.

In the distance, a bird song fades
to the silence of the canyon walls
before I can name the sweet singer.
Perhaps the aria is only imagined.

The wind is soft in ponderosa pines,
a stream chuckles over ancient rocks,
then, the descending notes of a song
from a flute that is the canyon wren.

The Last Dragonfly of Summer

This morning, the first full day of fall,
a dragonfly flits around the back yard.
The first one in weeks, and perhaps
the last one this summer.
Short days and cold nights
mean less food for them.

I will miss their zooming flight,
their electric blue and green bodies,
their gossamer wings, the pure joy
they bring to my heart.

Beauty Found on Our Morning Walk

My dog leads us on our morning walk
and stops at a dark thing lying in the sun.
It doesn't move when he noses it, paws it,
nor when I nudge it gently with my foot.

I recognize it as a cicada's husk, the empty
shell of that insect who fills summertime
trees with its song. I've not seen one up close,
so I pick it up and admire its pudgy body,
the black and white striping down its back,
green yoke around what would be its neck,
the olive green of its face, its small eyes
on arms out to the side and wonder if the
two black spots on its head are designed
to look like big eyes, to warn off predators.

I turn it over and beneath its six folded legs
I find the white striations of the tymbals,
sound boxes it uses to make and project
its mating song on hot August afternoons.
Under its front legs is a long beak, like a
humming bird's, used to sip sap from trees.

But it's the cicada's wings that hold my eye.
Transparent, longer than the body, they fold
over the back, like a Navy fighter's. Delicate,
parallel veins outline, give them substance,
wings that rival the dragonfly's gossamer.

Peaceful Morning's Walk

As I walk through October's
predawn stillness on a trail
through a small copse,
I sense that shadows around me
have assumed new shapes,
are no longer trees, are dense,
alert, breathing. I've walked
into a small herd of elk.

Nature guides me,
whispers to me,
"Keep walking. They
don't yet fear you
because you
don't yet fear them."

I exit the copse —
then fill with fear —
keep walking,
don't look back.

Fear slowly fades.

Night Sky, Sand Dunes, July 1987

My son and I lay out in sleeping bags
to stay warm in the cold desert night.
We let our eyes adjust to night's dark.
We have lived for years on the edge
of a small city's lights and he has never
seen the night sky this clear, this huge.

We are suddenly overwhelmed
by the shattering stillness of the night,
the cold light of the billions of stars.
We try to orient ourselves, look for
the big dipper, the north star, summer
triangle, Scorpio's red eye, curled tail.
They are lost in the night's brilliance.
We lay there silently, in raptured awe.

My son wishes that the thin veil
of high clouds across tonight's sky
weren't there so he can see better.
He's stunned to learn he sees clearly
for the first time the Milky Way.

This morning at breakfast he tells
me that he felt for a while last night
that he was adrift in that brilliant sky.
I tell him that our sun is one of those
dust motes in the Milky Way and we
were all adrift in last night's sky.

The Light on the First Day of September

When I wake now at five, morning has not yet come, stars
wink and a waning gibbous moon rides the still dark sky.

At five on the first of May, light in the east, announced that
the sun would soon bring up the day. The first low crocuses
had blown and tall tulips and daffodils had replaced them.

The light this morning has a lifeless quality of petals fallen
from roses in the garden, and light filtered through trees
to the south doesn't have that vital green tint of mid July.

Soon the sun drifts to that angle that tells trees to change
their shirts from green to orange, red, burnt umber, gold.

And this weakening of morning's light is a reminder that
my life's long past its September, summer's leaves turned,
the garden's dying hues of brown. The pace of my winter
speeds up much too quickly. December's dark mornings
will greet me at five, and its days will be cold and short.

About the Author

Art Elser is a poet and writer who has been published in many journals and anthologies. His books include a memoir, *What's It All About, Alfie?*, and four books of poetry, *We Leave the Safety of the Sea*, *A Death at Tollgate Creek*, *As The Crow Flies* and *To See a World in a Grain of Sand*. Art lives in Denver with his wife, Kathy, and their pup, Walker.

www.ingramcontent.com/pod-product-compliance
Lightning Source LLC
Chambersburg PA
CBHW020430010526
44118CB00010B/502